100 Questions and Answers About Chaldean Americans

I0192268

Michigan State University
School of Journalism

Front Edge Publishing

For more information and further discussion, visit
news.jrn.msu.edu/culturalcompetence/

Cover art and design by
Rick Nease
www.RickNeaseArt.com

Published by
Front Edge Publishing, LLC
42015 Ford Road, Suite 234
Canton, Michigan

Front Edge Publishing specializes in speed and
flexibility in adapting and updating our books. We
can include links to video and other online media. We
offer discounts on bulk purchases for special events,
corporate training, and small groups. We are able to
customize bulk orders by adding corporate or event
logos on the cover and we can include additional pages
inside describing your event or corporation. For more
information about our fast and flexible publishing or
permission to use our materials, please contact Front
Edge Publishing at info@FrontEdgePublishing.com.

Contents

Acknowledgments

The authors of this guide are these Michigan State University students. They are, front row from left: Whitney McDonald, Mattie Milne, Sakiya Duncan and Sierra Rehm; middle row from left: Alexea Hankin, Alexis Stark, Tiara Terry and Jesse Taconelli; back row, from left: Steven Maier, Josephine Boumis, Thor Mallgren, Zachary Robertson and Jessica Hanna. Motion graphics were produced by Alexa Seeger. Daniel Rayzel produced audio for the guide and motion graphics.

Wilson Sarkis, owner of Wilson Sarkis Photography & Cinematography, http://www. wilsonsarkisphotography.com contributed the photographs on the front and back covers.

We were blessed to have had a large group of knowledgeable allies who helped edit the questions and answers. Some began helping months before the class began and kept helping after it ended. Their oversight ensured the guide's accuracy and authority. Allies include:

Bishop Francis Y. Kalabat is the leader of the Chaldean eparchy that covers the eastern United States. It is based at Mother of God Church in Southfield, Michigan. Kalabat was previously pastor of St. Thomas Chaldean Catholic Church in West Bloomfield, Michigan, and studied at the University of San Diego's St. Francis de Sales Center for Priestly

Formation. Other clergy included **Father Pierre T. Konja**, administrator, and **Father Patrick Setto**, both at Mother of God Church, and **Father Manuel Boji**, pastor of Holy Martyrs Chaldean Catholic Church in Sterling Heights, Michigan.

Martin Manna is executive director of the Chaldean American Chamber of Commerce and president of the Chaldean American Foundation. He is also co-publisher of the Chaldean News. He invited us to chamber offices, answered questions and shared resources.

Vanessa Denha Garmo, who visited the class, is co-publisher and editor-in-chief of the Chaldean News. She is a communications strategist, media coach, producer and voice talent. She hosts community shows on AM and FM radio and founded Denha Media Group in 2009.

Dr. Zina Salem and **Jane Shallal** of the United Community Family Services (Chaldean American Ladies of Charity). Salem is CEO of the organization. She was founder and president of Chaldean Middle Eastern Social Services in El Cajon, California. Shallal is the organization's grants manager and was its executive director. She is an attorney, a professor and former president and CEO of the Associated Food and Petroleum Dealers.

Jacob Bacall is an entrepreneur, a leader of the Chaldean Iraqi American Association of Michigan and an author. He generously connected this project with many people in the community and was an enthusiastic supporter of its publication.

Mary Romaya, **Mariann Sarafa** and **Ann Rabban** opened the Chaldean Cultural Center to the class. We recommend a visit to this interactive museum.

Tom Alkatib, president, Chaldean Heritage Foundation, and **Amanda Alkatib**, Community Relations Specialist at UnitedHealthcare, provided advice even before the class began.

Judge Diane Dickow D'Agostini, 48th District Court, Oakland County, Michigan, responded quickly when asked for help.

State Rep. Klint Kesto, R-Commerce Township offered insight at the Michigan Capitol.

Detroit Free Press Assistant Metro Editor **Sally Tato** helped critique our work and gave it polish.

Joseph D. Sarafa, businessman, attorney and former director of the Associated Food and Petroleum Dealers, was an early adviser on the guide.

Margaret Saroki-Shamoun, chair of TEACH, an arm of Help Iraq, reviewed the questions and then the completed manuscript.

Dr. Adhid Miri with the Chaldean Community Foundation was a professor of chemistry at the University of Basrah, Iraq. He earned a bachelor of science in chemistry at the University of Baghdad and continued his studies at King's College and Brunel University in London.

Amer Hanna Fatuhi, artist, historian and designer, supplied information about his creation of a Chaldean flag.

Majid Kakka with Bells Band let us use music in the motion graphics. We invite you to watch them by using your cellphone to scan the square QR codes in the guide or by typing in the links.

MSU School of Journalism professor and director Lucinda Davenport offered her ongoing support for the series. Ann Hoffman, assistant dean for undergraduate education in the MSU College of Communication Arts and Sciences, made it possible for Seeger to make the motion graphics that appear with this guide. ✳

Foreword

By Weam Namou

Mesopotamia, known as the cradle of civilization and the land of milk and honey and now called Iraq, was home to the Chaldeans, Sumerians, Babylonians, Assyrians and Akkadians. It is the setting for much of the Old Testament, including the Garden of Eden, Adam and Eve, and the prophet Abraham. Some of the most significant developments or inventions credited to the Mesopotamians include writing, the wheel, agriculture, astronomy, mathematics, separation of time into hours, minutes, and seconds (the clock), irrigation, religious rites and beer. The first writer in recorded history was a woman from ancient Mesopotamia. Enheduanna, a princess, priestess and poet, wrote and taught about three centuries before the earliest Sanskrit texts, 2,000 years before Aristotle, and 1,700 before Confucius.

In "The Chaldean Account of Genesis," Assyria and Mesopotamia scholar George Smith discovered the "Epic of Gilgamesh" and translated it in 1876. He wrote, "The fragments of the Chaldean historian, Berosus, preserved in the works of various later writers, have shown that the Babylonians were acquainted with traditions referring to the Creation, the period before the Flood, the Deluge, and other matters forming parts of Genesis."

Yet for the most part, up until the 2003 U.S.-led invasion, Americans knew little about Iraq. Most didn't realize that it was associated with Mesopotamia and they were not aware of its contributions to our modern-day civilization. This was partly due to its name change from Mesopotamia after World War I, when the British created the Kingdom of Iraq in 1921.

I myself grew up not knowing much about my Chaldean heritage. In Baghdad, where I was born, schools didn't teach about history that occurred before Islam some 1,400 years ago. There were, however, selective history courses at universities that taught about ancient Mesopotamia. Chaldeans and Assyrians, having endured persecution under the Ottoman Empire and oppression in a war-torn land ruled by dictators, did not have the freedom or resources to keep their culture and heritage alive. For instance, they were discouraged from speaking in public their mother tongue, Sourath, which is a form of Aramaic. This wasn't the case in certain towns in the northern Iraq province of Mosul, which were almost exclusive to Christians.

The situation in northern Iraq dramatically changed in 2014 when the Islamic State invaded their villages and forced them out of the region. The attacks caused the Chaldeans, Assyrians and Syriacs in the United States to place greater efforts into assisting their relatives abroad as well as to preserve their stories, heritage and language.

Russian noblewoman Helena Petrovna Blavatsky wrote this about Chaldeans in her book "Isis Unveiled: Secrets of the Ancient Wisdom Traditions" (1877). "The ancients were always distinguished—especially the Chaldean astrologers and Magians—for their ardent love and pursuit of knowledge in every branch of science. They tried to penetrate the secrets of nature in the same way as our modern naturalists, and by the only method by which this object can be obtained, namely: by experimental researches and reason."

Ancient civilizations are important because they help us learn about and understand who we are. Telling their stories helps dispel stereotypes and brings people closer together. That's why "100 Questions and Answers about Chaldean Americans" by Michigan State University's School of Journalism is so important, especially since in the past decade, the United States has welcomed tens of thousands of Iraqi refugees, most of them to Michigan. We are all busy in our circles, but knowing our neighbors a little better could help us live a more peaceful life. ✱

Weam Namou is an Eric Hoffer Book award-winning author of 12 books, a filmmaker, journalist, and the vice president of Detroit Working Writers, a 118-year-old professional writing association. She also serves as Michigan ambassador of the Authors Guild of America.

Introduction: A New Home

By Jacob Bacall

When people ask me, "Who are Chaldeans?" and "Where is Chaldea?" I tell them Chaldeans are an ancient people and, of course, that Chaldea doesn't exist as a country but as a geographic place.

Chaldeans were the ancient inhabitants of Mesopotamia, presently known as Iraq, and made their home in the heart of the Fertile Crescent. The Chaldeans of Mesopotamia made enormous contributions to civilization. Hammurabi developed the first code of law, Nebuchadnezzar built the famous hanging Gardens of Babylon, they invented time instruments, the calendar, an alphabet and Aramaic, the "lingua franca" (bridge language) of the ancient world.

Chaldeans are Roman Catholic, having been converted to Christianity by St. Thomas. In the fifth century, Chaldeans espoused Nestorian doctrines until they were reunited with the church in Rome in 1552. Although Chaldeans are in union with Rome, they have their own patriarch. Chaldeans are strongly attached to their church not only for spiritual guidance, but also as the civil leader of the community.

A succession of wars, revolutions and religious and political prosecution of minority Christians pressured

Chaldeans and pushed them to leave their homeland for safety. The decision to leave home was never easy.

They experienced the challenges many immigrants face in learning a new language, finding a job and a place to live while adapting to a new culture. It was well worth the price, as it brought freedom, peace and a higher standard of living. While Chaldean Americans are proud of and sentimental about their roots, the United States is their home now.

When a small group of Chaldean Catholics left their village of Telkaif in northern Iraq on the route to the new world known as America, none had a clue that Detroit would become famous and the capital of the car-making industry and that people from all over the world would join them. This was the beginning of the Chaldean journey to America. Chaldean communities followed in California, especially the San Diego area cities of El Cajon, La Mesa and Rancho San Diego, in Arizona and in Chicago.

The Detroit metropolitan area has become the new capital of Chaldeans in the world. Beginning early in the 20th century, Chaldeans joined the long list of more than 50 ethnic groups that form the tapestry of Detroit.

The small Detroit Chaldean community attracted by Henry Ford's $5 day started buying small grocery stores and working long hours, employing family members. Almost every Chaldean immigrant could find a job with a relative working at a grocery store. They became a reliable labor force for the stores.

Chaldeans put their stamp on the city and surrounding community, operating 90 percent of the food stores in Detroit after the city's civil unrest of 1967. Those who came in the '60s, '70s, and '80s were known as "Baghdadians" because many were middle-class merchants from Baghdad.

In the greater Detroit area, their entrepreneurial business mentality earned them success and rapid growth. The majority of Chaldeans enjoy a higher standard of living and are thriving in their new land.

Many Chaldean immigrants who found these opportunities at grocery or liquor stores fell victim to crime. Records show that more than 200 Chaldean merchants have been slain by robbers or criminals since the 1970s.

Chaldeans have since made significant inroads into the hospitality business. They had experience in customer service and many owned hotels or inns in the Iraqi capital of Baghdad and other cities, such as Mosul and Basra. Others ventured into real estate, telecommunications, restaurants and fast-food franchises.

Chaldeans value both business and education. They first became entrepreneurs in retail, food and real estate. Chaldeans born in America are leaving the family grocery business for law, medicine, engineering and accounting. Today, males and females equally are seeking college and graduate school educations and professional careers.

The Chaldean Iraqi American Association of Michigan, which traces its roots to 1943, now has third- and fourth-generation members. In 1981, it opened the Southfield Manor, the first Chaldean social club in Michigan. It was a banquet facility with premier Middle Eastern cuisine.

Almost a decade after the manor's groundbreaking, club members recognized a golden opportunity in the availability of a neglected country club in West

Bloomfield, a growth area. Here was an opportunity to get the newer generation of Chaldeans engaged in golf, basketball and other recreational activities. On the last day of 1989, association members acquired the Shenandoah Country Club for $4.2 million.

By 2001, thanks to a successful banquet business and help from members, the manor and the club were debt-free. Stockholders approved the construction of a new Shenandoah Country Club at the estimated cost of $19 million.

As the association worked through building plan issues including drainage, wetlands, traffic and the size of the building, debate focused on adequate parking. The club is next to Temple Israel. Owing to their shared histories, Chaldean and Jewish communities in the Detroit area have always supported each other. The temple offered to share its parking lot to help its neighbor satisfy the township's parking concerns. The club would extend the same courtesy to the temple.

That October, a 90,000-square-foot club was built on the site of the old one. The new Shenandoah is a social and cultural center and houses the historically significant Chaldean Cultural Center museum.

But actual cost of construction was about $25 million, not including the land, which had been paid for before construction started. As the membership base increased to more than 1,200 members, higher dues and community support of the club banquet hall paved the road to achieve the goal.

Shenandoah, with its clubhouse, improved 18-hole golf course, athletic facilities, private member dining, mixed grill, ballroom, swimming pool and members' gym, has become a magnet to the younger generation and is open to the public.

The project was designed by Michigan architect Victor Saroki, whose ideas have also shaped St. Thomas Church and the Chaldean Foundation development.

Other organizations key to the community are the Chaldean American Ladies of Charity, founded in 1961, the Chaldean American Chamber of Commerce and Chaldean Foundation. Various Chaldean organizations have helped the community by offering counseling and assistance to small businesses and worked closely to build bridges among cultures.

Today, Chaldean Americans have embraced the mainstream society of the United States while retaining the rich cultural heritage of their ancestors. Having left a land of upheaval, Chaldeans have found a land of peace and stability and have prospered in it. While they are proud of and sentimental about their roots, they have built a new home. ✻

Jacob Bacall is an entrepreneur, community leader and author. Bacall Development, founded by Jacob Bacall and his brother Eddie, specializes in land development and property management, focusing on retail, office, apartments, hotel and congregate care projects. Jacob Bacall has written two illustrated books, "Chaldeans in Detroit" (2014) and "Chaldean Iraqi American Association of Michigan" (2018). He has served as president, vice president, treasurer and member of the association's board of trustees.

Introduction: Community Building

By Vanessa Denha Garmo and Martin Manna

Community building has been a priority for Chaldeans in America since they began arriving in the country.

A small group immigrated in the late 1800s. In the early 1900s, another group arrived.

In the 1960s, there was a large influx pulled by job security in the automotive industry in Michigan and pushed by uncertainty with the incoming Baath party of Saddam Hussein in Iraq.

The Iran and Iraq war of the 1980s prompted a new wave of immigration to the United States.

Over the years, community building has evolved to meet changing needs. Many groups and communication efforts from past generations have worked toward creating services and raising awareness.

Not only did leaders work toward educating people within the community, they also worked to educate non-Chaldeans. The leaders mobilized and created groups that focused on governmental relations, public relations and media awareness. Efforts were often coordinated through the Chaldean Catholic Diocese, business leaders and non-profit groups.

Educating local leaders and local media on who Chaldeans are and about our history required great effort and repeated conversations.

Chaldeans developed strong relationships with elected leaders such as U.S. Sen. Carl Levin, his brother, U.S. Rep. Sander Levin, Michigan governors Jim Blanchard and John Engler, as well as Detroit mayors Coleman A. Young, Dennis Archer and Mike Duggan.

Chaldeans also started building relationships to keep local media informed of issues and to better understand the community.

Community building really began to grow in the late 1990s and early 2000s.

In 2002, we began to brainstorm about creating a monthly magazine. The Chaldean News was two years in the making and debuted in February of 2004. We wanted to be part of building up our community and educating the broader audience about Chaldeans in America. At this same time, the Chaldean American Chamber of Commerce was being launched. It, too, grew out of a process and was in development for a while before launching. In 2006, the Chaldean Community Foundation was created as the non-profit arm of the chamber.

The chamber has collaborated with many outside entities to build the Chaldean community and educate the larger community. In 2008 and 2016, the chamber commissioned surveys about Chaldean households, businesses they own in Michigan and their economic impact on the state. The survey estimates more than 160,000 Chaldeans live in Michigan, contributing an estimated $11 billion annually to the economy.

The chamber has a strong government relations team that regularly meets with elected leaders in the state and the U.S. Congress on issues that affect Chaldeans in America and around the globe. As Chaldeans continued to be persecuted in the Middle East, there was another influx of immigrants from Iraq. Since 2007, more than 35,000 Chaldeans have arrived in the United States. The need to assist them assimilate into America became a priority and, through the efforts of the foundation, 30,000 people are served every year. More than 300,000 Chaldeans are still displaced throughout the Middle East.

This is all part of building community. We now have second-generation Chaldeans helping new immigrants find their way in America. ✳

Vanessa Denha Garmo, an award-winning journalist, is co-publisher and editor-in-chief of the Chaldean News. Martin Manna, co-publisher of the Chaldean News, is president and CEO of the Chaldean American Chamber of Commerce and the Chaldean Community Foundation.

Preface

One evening at the Shenandoah Country Club in West Bloomfield Township, Michigan, Jacob Bacall introduced me to Raad Kathawa, a retired grocer and a pillar in the Chaldean community. Kathawa asked how I became interested in Chaldeans.

It started in middle school.

I attended St. Bede's, a school in the Detroit suburb of Southfield. Not long after the U.S. Immigration and Nationality Act of 1965 opened doors to people from more countries, a new boy came to our school. The boy's name was Richard, and his family had come from Iraq. He was Catholic, like us, although he was Chaldean Catholic. He was the first person my own age I ever spent time with who was not, like me, of European descent.

I made Chaldean friends in high school. Later, as an editor at the Detroit Free Press, I listened as Chaldeans talked about our coverage of their community. As a parent, I sent my sons to school with the children of Chaldean parents. As a professor, I worked with Chaldean students in the classroom. I met for dinner with community members at the Southfield Manor and at Mother of God Church and was a wedding guest there for a student who came to work with me at the newspaper. She helped on this guide.

For more than 50 years, I have known Chaldean Americans. Many of their families fled their homeland to escape discrimination and persecution for a fresh start. The United States is their hoped-for forever home now. When, in 2017, the United States decided to deport Iraqi nationals, including Chaldeans, in exchange for dropping Iraq from a travel ban, I felt we needed this guide. While the guide was in production, one federal judge ordered that the Chaldeans not be deported. Then an appeals judge overruled that. The situation was still unsettled. Whichever way the detention issue is resolved, it revived old stereotypes.

The Detroit area, home to the largest population of Chaldeans in the United States, is the ideal place to build this bridge. The Bias Busters project in Michigan State University's Journalism School is the best way I have to do that. In working with my students on this guide, I have learned more about Chaldeans this year than I learned in the previous 50. I hope it is helpful to you, too. ☀

Joe Grimm
Series editor
Visiting editor in residence
Michigan State University School of Journalism

Identity

1 Who are the Chaldean people?

The Chaldean people trace their roots to ancient Babylon in what is now Iraq. Chaldeans are Catholics and a religious minority in Iraq, which is officially and predominantly a Muslim country. Most Chaldeans have left Iraq, primarily for the United States. Because they are widely dispersed, Iraq still has more Chaldeans than any other country. The Chaldean diaspora is especially present in North America, Australia, Europe and several countries in the Middle East.

2 How is "Chaldean" pronounced?

The phonetic spelling is Kal-de'an. The "Ch" is pronounced like the letter "k," as in kind. Then say "al," like the first part of alpha. Then pronounce the "d" as the letter is said, "dee." Finish with "in." (To hear people say Chaldean, scan this square image with a Quick Response Code reader in your cellphone, or type in the link. Either way will take you to the audio. Other QR codes in this book will let you watch motion graphics.)
https://soundcloud.com/joe-grimm/chaldeans

3 Are Chaldeans an ethnic group or a race?

Chaldeans are an ethnic group. Like any ethnic group, there is diversity within it. Primary characteristics that bind them and distinguish them from others in the Middle East are the Chaldean Catholic Church, their language and culture.

4 Do Chaldeans identify as White?

Most Chaldeans check the White or "other" box in the U.S. Census, according to the 2006 Detroit Arab American Study. This is how the U.S. government classified people from the Middle East. However, many Middle Eastern people in the United States have asked for a choice other than White. The Census Bureau said it would add a category for "Middle Eastern and North African" for the 2020 Census. This was canceled in 2018.

5 Are Chaldeans Arabs?

No. The Chaldean language is a dialect of Aramaic, not Arabic, which is a key identifier of Arabs. While Chaldeans share origins and some traditions with Arabs, their religion, language, culture and history make them distinct. Many Chaldeans identify as Catholic Iraqis or "Middle Eastern," which is geographic rather than cultural.

6 What are distinctions among Chaldeans, Assyrians and Syriacs?

Although all three have roots in the same region, they are religiously distinct. They also have linguistic, historic and cultural differences. Syriac is a language that also evolved from Aramaic, but is not Chaldean. Assyrians and Syriacs are Orthodox Christians and do not follow the pope. Chaldeans do.

7 Does Chaldea still exist?

No. Although people refer to a Chaldean nation in the sense of identity and heritage, there is no Chaldean country or government. Chaldea began as an ancient state in present-day southern Iraq and expanded greatly through conquest. The Chaldean Empire lasted from about 625 to 540 Before Common Era. It ended when the Persian Empire conquered Babylon.

8 Is the Chaldean identity in danger of vanishing?

Like many people, Chaldeans worry about the survival of their identity, religion, language and culture. With their homeland population greatly reduced, they face the challenges of keeping identity and tradition alive among people in new lands. Chaldean people are working to preserve their identity within other cultures. Some worry that marriage to non-Chaldeans will dilute them. In

2017, Chaldean Catholic bishops urged their people, particularly those who had left Iraq, to persevere and to hold onto their Chaldean faith and identity. ☀

Origins

9 Where was Chaldea?

Chaldea existed from around the late 10th or early 9th century until the mid-6th century Before Common Era. It covered much of present-day Iraq and Syria. The adjective Chaldean refers to Semitic descendants of ancient Babylon.

10 What have been Chaldean contributions to learning and knowledge?

Chaldeans and their predecessors, the Babylonians, made major contributions in writing, science, technology, mathematics and astrology. They devised the time system we use today with its 60-second minutes and 60-minute hours. They also described the circle as having 360 degrees. Their understanding of astronomy and ability to predict movements of heavenly bodies sparked what some have called the first scientific revolution. Across the ancient world, Greeks and Romans used the very name "Chaldean" for the astronomers of Mesopotamia.

11 How did they advance civilization?

Their ancestor, Hammurabi, created one of
the first legal codes in the world. Babylon was
known for architectural achievement including
its Processional Way and the hanging gardens,
one of the Seven Wonders of the Ancient World.
Nebuchadnezzar II greatly extended the empire to
Syria, Palestine, Judah and Jerusalem. In those times
of conquest, he also rebuilt Babylon and fortified
it. A prominent feature of the city was a 6th century
gate decorated with blue-glazed brick dedicated to
the goddess Ishtar. The gate, now a centerpiece at
the Pergamon Museum in Berlin, was decorated
with bulls symbolizing Ishtar, and dragons and lions
representing the gods Marduk and Adad. Situated
at the center of a major crossroads of trade and
development, Chaldean influences spread widely.

12 If Chaldeans are Catholics, why do they have these other gods?

These gods are from Babylonian times, which
predated Christ. Chaldeans were some of the first
converts to Christianity. While these gods are part
of their heritage and history, Chaldeans have not
followed them for a long time.

The Chaldean homeland

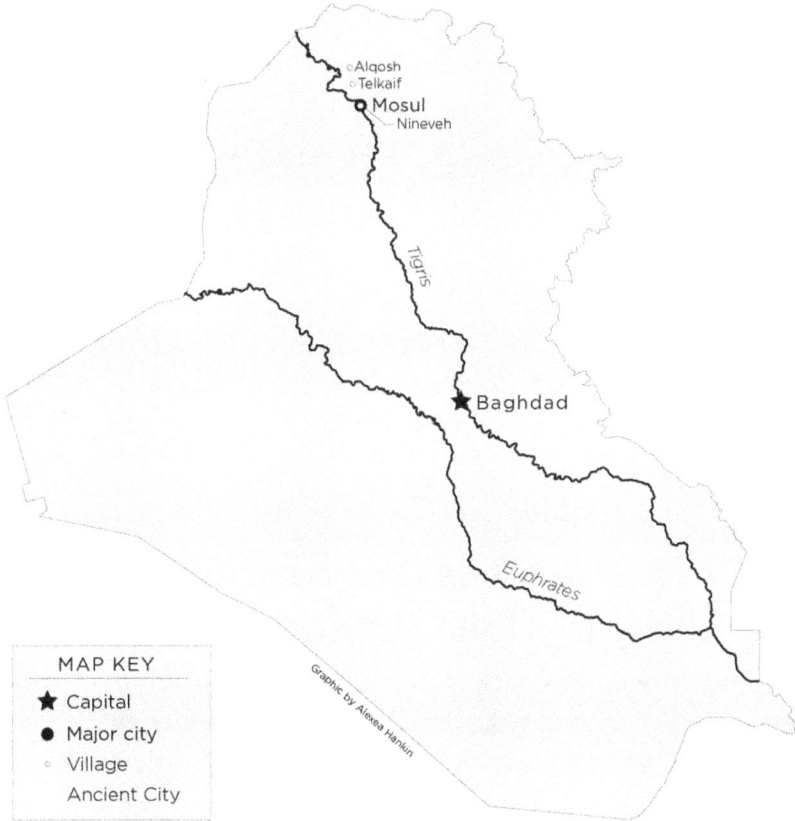

Alqosh
Telkaif
Mosul
Nineveh

Tigris

Baghdad

Euphrates

Graphic by Alexea Hankin

MAP KEY
★ Capital
● Major city
○ Village
Ancient City

Source: Chaldean American Chamber and Chaldean Community Foundation, 2018

13 Where are Chaldean Americans from specifically?

Chaldeans come from many villages and a few cities in what is now northern Iraq. Early Detroit settlers came from a northern village called Tel Keppe, Telkaif and other names. Over the past few decades, Tel Keppe has become primarily Muslim. More recent immigration has come from other places including Batnaya, Al-Qush, Tesqopa, Baqufa and Aradan. These lie between the Euphrates and Tigris rivers in an area bordered by Syria and Turkey.

14 Do Chaldeans still live in Iraq?

Yes, although their population has been greatly reduced, and the country now is about 97 percent Muslim. Remaining Chaldeans are a religious minority and targets of discrimination and even persecution by the government, warring factions and extremists. Chaldeans began leaving Iraq in much larger waves after 2003.

15 How did Chaldeans become a minority in a land they once ruled?

Christianity, Islam and Judaism once co-existed in the area. Acceptance broke down during centuries of conquest, religious and ethnic rivalries, politics and terrorism. At the time of the Islamic conquest in 634 A.D., most Iraqi tribes were Chaldean. Baghdad became the cultural center of the Muslim world. Later, it was occupied by the Mongols, followed by the Ottomans. The British took control in 1914-1917. In 1921, during British occupation, the Islamic Hashemite Kingdom of Iraq was founded. The name of the kingdom refers to Hashim, great-grandfather of the prophet Muhammad, to whom the dynasty traces its roots. Muslim governments have pushed Chaldean people to the margins for generations. Iraq

TWO WAVES OF IMMIGRATION

View video at:
https://www.youtube.com/
watch?v=b0tXEj4l9NE

gained independence from the British in 1932. In 1958, military officers overthrew the monarchy and Abd al-Karim Qasim was installed as president. In 2014, ISIS extremists seized parts of Syria and Iraq and persecuted Chaldeans and other religious minorities such as Yazidis and Mandaeans.

16 What significance does the homeland hold?

The Chaldean homeland is of great significance to its people and the world. The area is known as the Cradle of Civilization. To Chaldeans, their homeland is the place of ancestors and the wellspring of their identity. Many Chaldeans have relatives, ancestors and even claims to land in Iraq. However, returning can be difficult and dangerous. At Mass, a prayer for religious freedom reflects the importance of the homeland. The words are, "Bring harmony between church and states, put the end to wars on earth, and disperse the nations that desire war so that we may live a peaceful and calm life, in purity and fear of God."

17 When did the modern Chaldean identity emerge in the United States?

The number of Chaldean immigrants in the United States increased in the late 1960s, early 1970s and during the Iraq/Iran war of the 1980s. Chaldean American visibility and identity became more established as religious, social and business institutions grew. ✸

Immigration

18 Why did Chaldeans leave Iraq?

Going back, Chaldeans left Iraq for two main reasons: economic opportunity and religious freedom. Chaldeans left self-sufficient, non-industrialized farming villages for higher-paying jobs in the cities or abroad. Some migrated to Iraqi cities first and then moved out of the country. As religious discrimination, unrest and lack of government stability increased, people began migrating for safety and to practice their faith.

19 How many Chaldeans are there worldwide and where are they?

The Chaldean diaspora and the way censuses are conducted make this hard to pin down. One estimate comes from the Annuario Pontifico, the annual report of the Holy See at the Vatican. Its 2016 edition listed 23 jurisdictions for Chaldean Catholics worldwide. The population in the districts for that year totaled 640,828. The largest concentrations, in order, were in Iraq, the United States, Turkey, Australia, Canada, Lebanon, Syria, Jordan, Egypt and Iran. Other Chaldeans live in areas that do not have churches.

20 When did Chaldeans begin coming to the United States?

Chaldeans arrived in America as early as 1889, and the first wave began shortly before 1910. U.S. immigration laws changed in the 1920s, restricting Iraqi immigrants to 100 a year. This substantially decreased the number of Chaldeans arriving annually. Migration from Iraq largely stopped during World War II. Afterward, student visas were introduced, which allowed students to come study with the assumption they would return home with their knowledge. Many ended up marrying and stayed permanently. In 1965, U.S. law changed again, and immigration from many places, including Iraq, increased. The 1990-1991 Gulf War brought new restrictions. Immigration was also restricted by the Donald Trump administration.

21 What are U.S. population centers for Chaldeans?

The Chaldean American Chamber of Commerce reports "Metro Detroit has the world's largest population of Chaldeans outside of Iraq, with an estimated 121,000 people. Another 150,000 Chaldeans/Assyrians reside throughout the United States, particularly in the Chicago, San Diego and Phoenix areas." The 2016 annual directory of the Catholic Church's Holy See listed St. Thomas the Apostle Eparchy as the largest in the world with 180,000 members. It is centered in metro Detroit and covers the eastern United States. A 2018 report commissioned by the Chaldean Community Foundation estimated the Chaldean population in southeast Michigan between 155,000 and 160,000.

22 What immigration pattern did Chaldeans follow?

Chaldeans generally followed family or people from their village. Traditionally, men were the first to come to the United States. Once the men settled, other family members followed. Earlier immigrants then helped later arrivals with jobs, housing and advice. This chain migration has been followed by many immigrant groups to reunite families.

23 Do Chaldeans help other Iraqi refugees and immigrants?

Although the flow of Chaldean immigrants has slowed, Iraqi immigration in general has increased. Many fled ISIS. The Chaldean Community Foundation in suburban Detroit reports that demand for its services and assistance has spiked. It went from 16,000 people in 2016 to more than 26,000 in 2017. It was on pace to hit 30,000 in 2018. Newcomers are now more likely to be refugees. They arrive with more trauma and greater needs for counseling and training. The foundation also helps people from Arab countries including Syria, Lebanon and Egypt.

24 Are there differences among people from villages and those from cities?

A small, non-industrialized village, Telkaif had higher concentrations of Chaldeans than cities such as Mosul or Baghdad. People from villages were more likely to have worked in agriculture or small family businesses and to have lived in Sourath-speaking communities. Those from cities generally had more education, more professional experience and less immersion in Sourath.

25 Do Chaldean Americans have divided loyalties?

Although Chaldeans feel ties to their homeland, many fled to the United States to escape oppression and discrimination there. They say that returning to Iraq would be dangerous. Some who have made the trip back say it was heartbreaking. While they may long for their homeland, the one they remember no longer exists. Their lives are now rooted in the United States. ✴

Faith and Religion

26 What religion do Chaldeans practice?

Most Chaldeans are members of the Eastern Rite Chaldean Catholic Church. As such, they share key beliefs of the Catholic tradition. Chaldean churches have their own patriarch, practices and rituals. The Chaldean Catholic Church dates to shortly after the death of Jesus. There are more than a dozen Eastern rites of the Catholic Church. Some others are Syrian, Maronite, Armenian, Coptic, Ethiopian and Melkite. Each rite includes several churches.

27 What are some core tenets of Chaldean religious practice?

For Chaldean Catholics, the foundation is professed in statements of faith including the Apostles Creed and the Nicene Creed. They believe there is one God with three parts: Father, Son and Holy Spirit. They believe God created the Earth. They believe Jesus Christ was the Son of God and venerate Mary as the

Mother of God in the form of Jesus. His resurrection and ascension into Heaven are celebrated on Easter. They believe God offers forgiveness of sins and eternal life. All Catholics have practices rooted in these beliefs.

28 What are differences between Chaldean Catholicism and Eastern orthodoxy?

Both descended from the churches that developed under the reign of the Eastern Roman Empire. In the centuries after Jesus' time, Chaldean and Eastern Orthodoxy began to separate. They split over questions such as, "who was Jesus?" and "what does it mean to be the Son of God?" Eastern orthodoxy is the largest group that splintered from the eastern churches. The Assyrian Church of the East, from which Chaldeans separated, was a much smaller splinter. Today, Chaldean and Eastern Orthodox rituals and services have theological, cultural and language differences.

29 How is the Chaldean Catholic tradition unique?

Chaldeans and other Catholics agree on the major issues. They share beliefs and doctrines but differ in prayers and the order of services. Another difference is that Chaldeans receive confirmation soon after being baptized as infants, rather than around age 14.

The major holidays of Easter and Christmas are celebrated at the same time, but some holidays occur on different days.

30 What are differences in holidays?

Chaldeans begin Lent on Monday rather than Ash Wednesday. They also have a three-day fast of Nineveh, remembering the three days Jonah spent in the whale. It was first observed to break a plague. Another Chaldean tradition is observance of Jan. 6 or a weekend near it for baptisms. This mirrors when Christ was baptized. Parents whose children are born late in the year might wait for Jan. 6 to have them baptized.

31 Do Chaldeans fast?

Chaldean Catholics fast on most Fridays and for the three-day pre-Lenten observance of Ba'utha, which is explained near the end of this guide. Fasting Chaldeans abstain from food for all or some periods of the day, or give up other activities or comforts. Many set aside more time for prayer. Fasting is suspended for times of celebration such as Easter and Christmas.

32 What is the pope's relationship to the Chaldean Catholic Church?

Chaldeans and their patriarch, the head of the Chaldean Catholic Church, recognize the pope as the ultimate church authority. Chaldean Catholics operated separately from the Catholic Church for centuries, but were unified beginning in the 16th century. Pope Julius III recognized the Chaldean Catholic Church in 1553. The churches came into full union in 1830.

33 How are Chaldean Catholics and Assyrians different?

Chaldean Catholics and members of the Assyrian Church of the East originated in Iraq, but have separate hierarchies. Chaldean Catholics were members of the Church of the East before they joined Catholicism. The Church of the East doesn't recognize the authority of the pope. The groups pray and schedule services differently, and have doctrinal differences on several points, including details surrounding Jesus' relationship to God the Father. However, both churches face similar challenges.

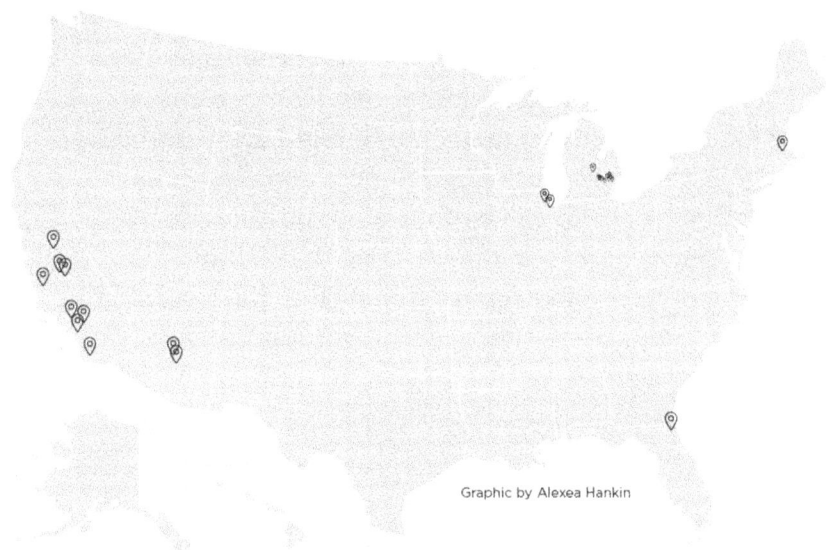

Graphic by Alexea Hankin

34 How is the Chaldean Catholic Church organized in the United States?

The pope is at the top of the Chaldean hierarchy. He is followed by the Chaldean patriarch in Baghdad, who appoints bishops to lead the two Chaldean dioceses in the United States. The Eparchy of St. Thomas the Apostle, based in southeast Michigan, serves the eastern United States. The Eparchy of St. Peter the Apostle is based in San Diego and serves western states. Those bishops oversee priests presiding over the churches in their regions.

35 Do most U.S. Chaldeans attend church?

A 2008 survey conducted by the Chaldean Chamber of Commerce in Detroit found that 59.4 percent of Chaldean people attended church regularly. Another 33.4 percent said they attended occasionally. Some attend non-Chaldean Catholic churches and receive sacraments there. For comparison, the Gallup polling organization reported that church attendance among U.S. Catholics in general around that time was 45 percent.

36 Can people become Chaldean through religious conversion?

People can convert, but this does not change their ethnic identity. Even people who attend a Chaldean church, marry into the Chaldean community and convert do not become ethnically Chaldean.

37 Do women cover their hair in Chaldean churches?

It is not required and most do not. Some more traditional women choose to wear veils or scarves. An article in the National Catholic Reporter noted that Catholic canon law called for women to cover their heads in 1917, but dropped the rule in 1983. The reasons for covering hair appear to be for modesty and respect, like the reasoning in some other religions. The article noted that some traditionalists were reviving the custom.

38 Do Chaldeans practice their religion in Iraq?

The Chaldean patriarch remains in Iraq. The seat of the Chaldean Catholic Church is the Cathedral of Mary Mother of Sorrows in Baghdad. The annual directory of the Catholic Church's Holy See lists dioceses in several other Iraqi cities including Mosul, Basra, Erbil and Kirkuk.

39 Are there other religious minorities in Iraq?

Yes. According to the Middle East Research and Information Project in Washington, D.C., the Iraqi census counted 1.4 million Christians there in 1987. In 2003, there were an estimated 1 million. Today, some church officials say the number is as low as 500,000. Two-thirds of these Christians belong to the Chaldean tradition. The next largest group is the Assyrian Church of the East, also known as the Nestorian Church. It has 170,000 members in Iraq, Syria and Iran. The Melkite Catholic Church is another, alongside the Syriac Catholic and Orthodox churches and Armenian Eastern Rite churches. A Kurdish speaking group, the Yazidi, practice a blend of pre-Islamic Assyrian traditions, Islam, Christianity and Zoroastrianism. Though very few remain, one of the oldest Jewish communities in the world is in Iraq. ✺

There is more information on Chaldean religious holidays at the back of this guide.

Language

40 What is the Chaldean language?

Chaldeans speak Sourath, a dialect known in English as Aramaic. Sourath is in the Afro-Asiatic family of Semitic languages. That includes Hebrew, Arabic, Akkadian, Ethiopic and Phoenician. Aramaic is closely related to Hebrew and Arabic. Some use Aramaic and Chaldean interchangeably as names for the language. The term Sourath is used less frequently.

41 Do Chaldeans speak the language of Jesus?

Chaldeans call Aramaic, the language of ancient Babylon, the oldest continuously spoken language in the world. Using and preserving the language Jesus used is seen as a special responsibility. Although the dialect has evolved, Chaldeans take pride in speaking and worshipping in Aramaic. It also confirms their status as an ancient people.

42 What language do Chaldean children learn to speak at home?

Chaldean children in families from Iraq might speak dialects of Aramaic as well as Arabic and English. This depends on where their family came from and what is spoken at home. As Chaldean Americans grow up and spend time with extended family members or friends, they might learn additional languages. Children are generally less likely than their parents' generation to learn Aramaic at home.

43 Why do some Chaldeans also speak Arabic?

Arabic is the official language in Iraq and is used in public school, business and government. It would be difficult to live in the region without speaking and writing Arabic. So many Chaldeans know Arabic that some Chaldean Catholic churches offer services in Arabic, as well as Aramaic and English.

44 Is the Aramaic language endangered?

In Chaldean, "Lushan d Youmma Knater A'amma" means "Mother's tongue keeps the nation alive." Persecution of Chaldeans in Iraq and their diaspora to countries of different languages has threatened their own tongue. The Detroit area's Chaldean American Chamber of Commerce, the Chaldean Community Foundation and Mango Languages have collaborated on preservation. They have created a series to teach Sourath. The biggest challenge has been finding experts fluent in English and Aramaic to help write lessons.

45 How is the language written?

Aramaic has 22 letters and is written right to left. Aramaic uses the abjad writing system, which means each symbol represents a consonant. Vowels can be marked in the writing but often are not. ✸

Culture

46 How have Chaldeans acculturated in the United States?

The challenge for many groups is to acculturate without being assimilated and losing one's identity. This is a special concern for Chaldeans, whose identity must be sustained in their adopted countries. Every immigrant group struggles between maintaining its cultural identity while adjusting to new customs. In the United States, Chaldeans are helped by those who came before them. This is one reason people settle in ethnic communities. Institutions such as the church and business associations anchor them.

47 What is traditional Chaldean dress?

In traditional villages, men and women wore modest, loose, ankle-length robes suited to the climate. The robe is called a dishdasha or dishdashi. Women and children's garments might be decorated with embroidery and beads. There is no singular style. Colors and decoration could identify a person's village. Similar garments are traditional in other

WHO ARE THE CHALDEAN PEOPLE?

View video at:
https://www.youtube.com/
watch?v=eZbW1l7Yxuo

Middle Eastern countries. In the United States, Chaldeans dress like other Americans. In modern Iraqi cities, contemporary clothing is the fashion.

48 What is the Chaldean flag?

The flag is a modern creation designed in 1985 by Amer Hanna Fatuhi. Blue vertical lines signify the Tigris and Euphrates rivers, which ran through ancient Babylon. A red, eight-pointed star dates to 6,000-year-old pictographs and represents Babylonian law and justice. A yellow circle symbolizes the sun, and a blue circle within is for the moon. Together, they stand for Chaldean contributions in human history, particularly in astronomy and math.

Chaldean Flag
ܢܝܫܐ ܕܟܠܕܝܐ
علم الكلدان

49 What is the connection between Chaldeans and Jews?

There are many kinds of connections. Martin Manna, president of the Chaldean American Chamber of Commerce, says the communities have lived together since Babylonian times. Detroit area Chaldeans and Jews are neighbors, they collaborate on community building and worship near each other. The publisher of the Detroit Jewish News, Arthur Horwitz, echoes Manna. He told Metromode, "Both had a common history of having their rights constrained or restricted, not having the ability to own property." Manna and Horwitz have forged an ongoing "Building Bridges" initiative and the Jewish

News and the Chaldean News co-publish content. Furthermore, the Chaldean Community Center highlights connections between the two Semitic communities. Manna said Chaldeans have bought Jewish businesses, and Jews have protested the detentions of Chaldeans.

50 Who are some well-known Chaldeans in the United States?

Bishop Ibrahim N. Ibrahim was chosen to start the American branch of the Chaldean Catholic Church in 1985. He did so at the Chaldean Eparchy of St. Thomas the Apostle in Southfield, Michigan.

Bishop Francis Y. Kalabat succeeded Ibrahim in 2014. Kalabat was previously pastor of St. Thomas Chaldean Catholic Church in West Bloomfield, Michigan, and had studied in San Diego.

Bishop Sarhad Yawsip Hermiz Jammo founded the Eparchy of St. Peter the Apostle, with headquarters in San Diego. It covers 19 western states.

Justin Meram was the first Chaldean athlete in Major League Soccer, playing for the Columbus Crew and Orlando City.

Michael J. George, the Detroit-born businessman son of a Chaldean farmer, co-founded Melody Farms Dairy Co. and the Chaldean Iraqi American Association of Michigan. The dairy became one of the largest private dairy and beverage distribution companies in the state. George, who died in 2017, helped set up scores of Chaldeans in the retail business.

Victor Saroki is an award-winning architect who designed the Shenandoah Country Club in West Bloomfield. He is a graduate of Lawrence Technological University and was honored by the Chaldean American Chamber of Commerce as Business Person of the Year in 2017.

The **Jonna Family** of Metro Detroit exemplifies entrepreneurship at a high level. Arkan, Frank, Eddie and Joseph Jonna have a network of retail, residential, business and gourmet market operations that spans more than 30 states.

Raad Ghantous is an interior designer known particularly for his work at the Cultural Center in San Clemente, California.

Dr. Mona Hanna-Attisha is a pediatrician credited with publicizing the problem of lead-tainted drinking water in Flint, Michigan. She compared children's blood test results with those from children in nearby areas and then fought state officials who denied the problem. Her book about the crisis is "What the Eyes Don't See: A Story of Crisis, Resistance, and Hope in an American City."

Sabri Shamoun turned the earnings from a small store in Detroit into a multimillion-dollar real estate venture in San Diego.

Yasmine Hanani's acting credits include "Voices of Iraq," "My Country, My Country" and "The Blood of My Brother." ☀

Food

51 What are some Chaldean food traditions?

Eating is to Chaldean families as salt is to food. Food brings families together and reminds them of God's blessings and the continuity of life. Traditional foods include citrus, melons, green beans, squash, okra, eggplant, lentils, onions, wheat, barley, grapes, olives and olive oil, pomegranates, figs and dates. Cattle, sheep and goats provide meat, and milk for cheese. River fish are part of the diet, too. Spices described in recipes dating back to Mesopotamia flavor kabobs, meat and vegetable stews, and dishes are served with rice or bread. Dates and nuts flavor desserts. Proximity and similarities in climate and soil mean Chaldeans, Persians, Turks and Greeks have influenced each other.

52 How is Chaldean food distinct from other Middle Eastern cuisine?

Several foods are widespread throughout the Middle East. Kabobs, kufta, Greek souvlaki and Russian shashlik are similar to each other. Shawarma, gyros and doner kebab are also alike. Hummus and stuffed grape leaves are widespread. Distinctive names, seasonings, cuts and methods of preparation can be regional or local. Villages and even families became known for their interpretations of popular foods. Chaldeans have no religious restrictions against pork, but with consumption discouraged by the majority Muslim population in Iraq, pork is largely unavailable and does not play a large role in Chaldean cuisine.

53 What are some traditional Chaldean foods?

Kuba is a flat, round bread 8 to 15 inches across, filled with meat and spices or almonds and raisins.

Kuzi is a seasoned lamb dish roasted with pine nuts and almonds, raisins and cow or goat butter. This is served at special occasions such as baptisms, communions, engagements and weddings and is often accompanied with rice.

Pakota or **habbiyah** is a barley dish made with onion and seasoned with turmeric. It is bright yellow with a creamy texture.

Gurgur or bulgur is a cracked wheat cereal that predated rice for Chaldeans and is a mealtime staple.

Masgouf is a fish cooked with dried limes, called **numi bussra**, and topped with tomato and curry.

Kharoof mahshi is roasted lamb stuffed with rice and nuts.

54 What are some Chaldean desserts?

Popular desserts include **kolache**, or **kleicha, geymer** and **kahi**. Kolache is a cookie served with tea and eaten during holidays such as Christmas and Easter. It is filled with crushed walnuts, coconut or kneaded dates. Geymer is clotted cream made with water and buffalo milk, which gives it a creamy texture. It is often served with flatbread. Kahi, a buttery phyllo dough filled with custard, is traditionally eaten as breakfast or dessert.

55 How are holiday meals served?

Chaldeans celebrate Easter, Christmas and American Thanksgiving with **dolma**: grape leaves stuffed with rice, meat, tomato paste, onion and spices. Iraqi dolma is distinctive for including vegetables such as cabbage, green or red peppers, eggplant, zucchini and cucumber. A classic Chaldean food for Thanksgiving and Christmas is **pacha**. It is made with cow or sheep intestine and stomach lining stuffed with rice and beef or lamb.

56 What is the role of tea or coffee in Chaldean hospitality?

With variations, tea is an important drink in many cultures. Chaldeans serve strong, black, sweet tea and dessert to guests. If you are offered tea or coffee, it is good manners to accept this hospitality. Tea is traditionally served in a small glass called an istican. It is common to socialize over two or three cups at a meeting or meal. ✳

Chaldean Recipes

These recipes are from "Ma Baseema: Middle Eastern Cuisine with Chaldean Flair." They are printed here with the permission of the publisher, the Chaldean American Ladies of Charity. "Ma Baseema" means "How good it is!" The book is available from the publisher, listed in the resources section of this guide, and from Amazon.

Chaldean Allspice Blend "Baharat"

Cook: Mary Shallal

2 ½ pounds ground black pepper
1 ¼ pounds ground allspice
1 pound ground cloves
1 pound ground cinnamon
¼ pound ground cardamom (hale)
½ pound ground nutmeg
½ pound edible, food-grade rose petal powder
(Edible rosebud powder may be substituted.)

Mix all ingredients together and store in jars in a cool, dark place.

Preparation time: 15 minutes
Makes: 7 pounds

Why so much spice? Chaldean cooks make large quantities of spice to store some and share some with family and friends, a sign of hospitality.

Beef Chil-Fry

Cook: Najibah Kirma

Chil-Fry, also known as "Pusra Kuilleya" are tender pieces of beef sautéed with onions and tomatoes and it is a popular breakfast meal in Iraq. The term "chil-fry" describes chilled foods (tomatoes and meat) being fried or sautéed.

1 ½ pounds chuck roast, cut into cubes
½ teaspoon salt
1 tablespoon olive oil
2 medium Spanish onions, diced
1 large green pepper, diced (optional)
½ teaspoon ground pepper or allspice (Baharat)

Warm breads to serve

Flavor meat with salt. In large skillet heat olive oil over high heat and add seasoned meat. Stir and mix to keep meat from burning. When meat is halfway cooked add onions, green pepper (optional) and ground pepper (or allspice). Reduce heat to medium and continue to mix. When meat is thoroughly cooked, add tomatoes. Additional salt and pepper or allspice (Baharat) can be added to your liking.
Serve with warm bread (pita, toast, samoun).

Preparation time: 30 minutes
Cooking time: 30 minutes
Serves 3-4.

Ground Chicken Kabobs "Kufta 'd Kathatha"

Cook: Melody Delly

2 pounds ground chicken breast
1 cup chopped parsley
½ cup finely chopped onions
1 teaspoon salt
1 teaspoon garlic powder
1 teaspoon black pepper
½ teaspoon paprika
2 tablespoons all-purpose flour

Place all ingredients in a bowl and knead into a thick paste. Refrigerate for 1-2 hours.

Take about ¼ pound of ground chicken and mold into a sausage link shape onto a skewer. Place skewers over heated grill and cook chicken for about 5 minutes on each side or until done and meat is tender.

Remove cooked kabobs from skewers with pita bread and serve.

Preparation time: 20 minutes
Cooking time: 10-15 minutes
Makes: 8 kabobs or 4 servings

Variation: 3 crushed garlic cloves can be used instead of onions.

Families

57 What are Chaldean family values?

From her research, Wayne State University sociologist Mary Sengstock reported that the core values of the Chaldean community are church and family. Family ties are important in the development of individuals and their social circles, she wrote. Family serves an important role in immigration, church traditions, home and work.

58 How are Chaldean families structured?

In Iraq, the Chaldean family structure was patrilineal, descending from the male line. Typical households usually had members of the extended family and several generations. Couples often were from the same village. Today in the United States, there are many more types of family structures, and responsibilities are shared.

59 Is there a typical gender dynamic for Chaldean parents?

Family dynamics vary. Roles can be influenced by age, gender and income. Among early immigrants, men had to work or run businesses and women ran households. As families became established in the United States, distinct role separations blurred. In many families, dynamics and gender roles are a blend of Iraqi and U.S. culture. The length of time in the United States, the degree of acculturation and changes in the larger society are all factors, and people react to them in different ways.

60 How large are Chaldean families?

According to the 2008 Chaldean Chamber of Commerce Household Survey, 84 percent of Chaldean families in the Metro Detroit area had five or fewer members in the same house. Fifteen percent had more than five. The average household size had decreased slightly from the 2000 census. Ten years later, the Detroit-area Chaldean community survey showed 20 percent of homes had five or more people and 60 percent had three members under one roof.

61 Is there a main type of Chaldean household?

The 2018 Chaldean Community Foundation classified Chaldean households into four types:

- **Educated Middle Agers, 30 percent:** These households had people 40-60 years old, they were more likely to own businesses and spoke Chaldean. The head of the household was most likely an immigrant.
- **Adult Children Living at Home, 23 percent:** Ages ranged from 50 to 70. Most households did not have children under 18, and 89 percent had an Iraqi-born adult.
- **Young Families, born in the United States, 32 percent:** The average age was 36, and there were typically two parents at home.
- **Empty Nesters, 15 percent:** Averaging 77 years of age, immigrants were the heads of 94 percent of these households.

62 What is the role of elders in a family?

As with many groups, Chaldean elders historically are treated as keepers of culture and tradition. In immigrant families, these are the sources of knowledge about life and culture in Iraq. They also serve as teachers of traditional religion.

63 How do families care for elders?

Care for elderly Chaldean family members starts at home. The immediate family is largely responsible for the care of elders, with physicians providing skilled health care. Family members help with chores, meals, transportation and provide companionship. According to Sengstock, women typically help with cooking or housework for elders. Men assist with finances. Two Chaldean Catholic churches in the Detroit area have built adjacent housing complexes for older parishioners.

64 How do generational differences play out?

The degree to which individuals acculturate plays a big role in generational differences among Chaldean Americans. Iraqi-born immigrants keep Chaldean culture differently than American-born Chaldeans. While many Chaldean families maintain the culture and tradition, they are often mixed with practices in the United States. Culture does not stand still. It is changing in Iraq and the United States simultaneously. There can be friction within families as younger generations feel pulled toward American ideals and values. Older family members who want to protect their children and culture may feel threatened by this. Even members of the same family can disagree about how best to raise children, so there are no across-the-board answers about how differences are displayed.

65 Do families tend to be patriarchal or matriarchal?

In Iraq, the father or oldest male is the patriarch of the family. Female roles were to maintain the household and take care of children. Today in the United States there is more variety. The roles of head of house, caretaker and money manager can pass between males and females. Familial responsibilities and power are shared more equally.

66 Do Chaldeans have traditions for naming children?

Traditionally in Iraq, boys and some girls have names from their fathers and paternal grandfathers. A child's second name is the father's name. First-born sons receive the name of their father's father as a third name. The fourth name is the family name. Naming conventions like this are used elsewhere in the Middle East and help indicate lineage. The practice is less common in the United States.

67 Are expectations for sons and daughters the same?

Historically, there was greater pressure on daughters to marry young and within the culture. Sons were encouraged to get an education and help run the family business. While elements of these gender roles still exist, Chaldean families have expanded their expectations for education, career and marriage.

This comes from influences of American culture and generational differences. Each Chaldean family has its own expectations. ☀

Dating and Marriage

68 Is dating allowed in Chaldean families?

Yes, however, families set limits. People who are neither married nor engaged are traditionally not described as "boyfriends" and "girlfriends." Chaldean tradition is to have a period of courtship that leads to marriage, rather than to date many people. However, Chaldean people who grew up in the United States more frequently follow U.S. dating styles.

69 Do Chaldeans have arranged marriages?

Arranged marriage is far less common in the United States than it was in Iraq, although marriage is still a family affair. While people tend to choose their partners, it is usually done with some parental involvement. Rather than choose potential spouses for their children, parents might make introductions. Many Chaldean couples meet on their own and introduce their choices to their parents. Mutual agreement strengthens family ties.

70 How is intercultural marriage regarded?

Marrying in the community helps preserve the culture and assures that children will be raised within the Chaldean Catholic Church. Marriage to other Catholics is not unusual. Immigration to the United States has increased intermarriage. Living away from a Chaldean community increases the chances of intermarriage, so some families encourage children to stay close by.

71 How are engagements celebrated?

Traditionally, there were four steps toward marriage. The first two are now frequently combined. While traditional American engagements are private events that might happen after seeking parental permission, a Chaldean engagement is occasion for a celebration. It can include a priest performing a ceremony, followed by a party and professional photography of the couple.

1. The man comes with his close family members to the woman's house and asks her father for her hand in marriage.
2. The man and woman promise themselves to each other. During this small celebration, the families come together and the man places a piece of jewelry on the woman to indicate she's taken.

This is called "tenetha" in Sourath and "kilma" in Arabic and translates to "word."

3. The official engagement occurs.
4. The wedding.

72 What is a Chaldean wedding celebration like?

Chaldean wedding ceremonies, which could take several days, have changed. The religious ceremony may be small. It unites not just the couple, but two families in the presence of God. Wedding receptions tend to be large. There is a saying that when you marry a Chaldean, you marry the entire tribe. A large reception implies this. Wedding ceremonies and celebrations today blend American and traditional elements. One tradition is pre-wedding henna parties for women. Henna, or hinna, is an orange paste applied to the palms or painted on the hands, fingers or arms in elegant designs that turn reddish brown. Designs symbolize good luck and fortune. Brides typically wear a galabia, a long, colorful garment with beading and embroidery, at the henna party and a white dress for the wedding. In some weddings, the bride and groom wear ceremonial crowns. These represent Christ, the church and equality in their relationship. Another tradition is a high-pitched trilling women make during wedding receptions.

73 What is the Chaldean Catholic Church's position on divorce?

The Catholic Church generally does not recognize divorce. Under certain circumstances, the church will issue annulments, which declare a marriage was never valid. If people do not receive an annulment from a first marriage, they cannot get remarried in the Catholic Church. ☀

Work and Money

74 What fields do Chaldean people tend to work in?

The most common source of work among Chaldeans is entrepreneurship. The 2018 Chaldean Community Foundation report about Chaldeans in Michigan found that 58 percent said they owned a business. Thirty percent owned several. The businesses most commonly owned by Chaldeans were convenience stores, supermarkets, gas stations, construction, rental property and real estate.

75 What career expectations do Chaldean families have for their children?

Chaldean families' hopes for their children's careers vary. Some wish their children will stay in the family business. Others work so that their children can pursue educations and careers of their choice.

Chaldean business ownership

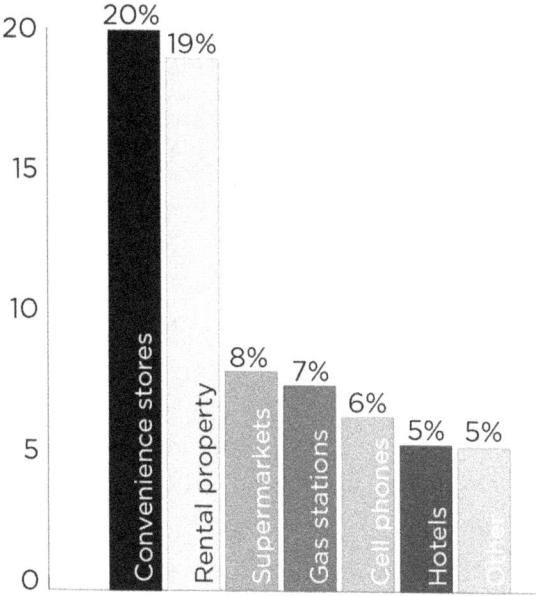

Source: *Chaldean American Chamber and Chaldean Community Foundation, 2018*
Graphic by Alexea Hankin

76 Are there generational differences in occupational choices?

Yes. First-generation Chaldean Americans primarily support themselves through business ownership, while the second and third generations have branched into other fields. Later generations are more likely to be dentists, lawyers, doctors, engineers, teachers and accountants. According to the Chaldean Community Federation's 2018 report, the generation aged 40-60 years had the most business owners. Younger generations typically receive more education than older family members and follow new career paths.

77 Are Chaldean businesses targets for crime?

Running small cash businesses such as convenience stores and gas stations that can be isolated and open late made Chaldeans vulnerable. More than 200 business owners have been killed in metro Detroit since the 1970s according to the Chaldean American Chamber of Commerce. This problem has been reduced through cross-cultural outreach and because Chaldeans are moving into other occupations. Business associations have increased security and vigilance, and trained business owners in communication and community relations.

78 Do Chaldeans support family members financially?

Many Chaldeans support their extended family by sharing resources. This was especially so for Chaldeans who were new to the country and making a fresh start. When a Chaldean immigrant arrived in the United States, family or community members hired them or helped them start businesses. This gave newcomers time to adjust and start making money. Once Chaldean immigrants got on their feet financially, they were expected to remain loyal to those who had helped them and to help the next wave of immigrants.

Household income

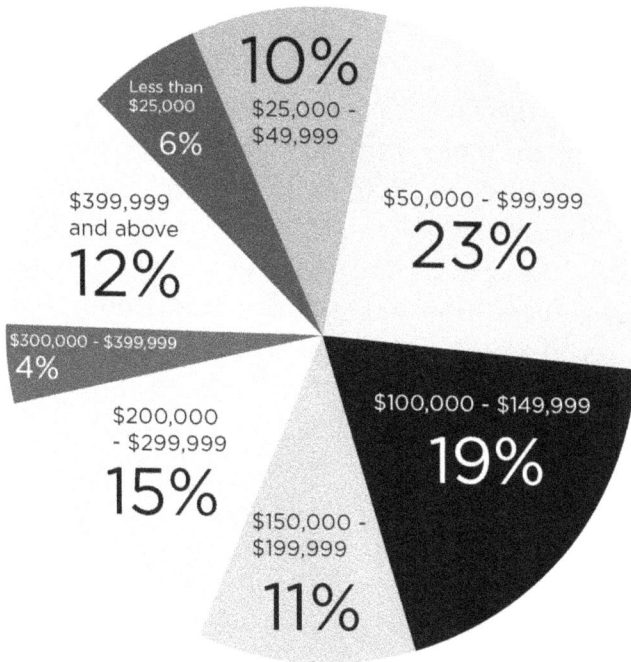

10%
$25,000 - $49,999

Less than $25,000
6%

$399,999 and above
12%

$300,000 - $399,999
4%

$200,000 - $299,999
15%

$150,000 - $199,999
11%

$50,000 - $99,999
23%

$100,000 - $149,999
19%

Source: Chaldean American Chamber and Chaldean Community Foundation, 2018

Graphic by Alexea Hankin

79 What is the average income for Chaldeans?

According to the 2018 report by the Chaldean Community Foundation, the median household income for Chaldeans in the Detroit area was $150,000 to $200,000.

80 Are there Chaldean charities?

Yes. One is the Chaldean Community Foundation.
Another is the United Community Family Services,
founded as the Chaldean American Ladies of Charity.
Another is the non-profit Adopt-a-Refugee Family
Program, founded in 2007 by hotel developer and
owner Basil Bacall. Charities that began by helping
Chaldean Americans have expanded their missions
to serve others. They offer scholarships, school
supplies, food, job training, refugee aid, language
lessons and help with disability issues. ☀

Education

81 Do Chaldean children attend non-Chaldean Catholic schools?

Many families send their children to Catholic schools because there are few Chaldean Catholic schools. In 2015, the nonprofit Keys Grace Academy was chartered in Madison Heights, Michigan. It is not a religious school. According to its website, the school emphasizes "the study of the Chaldean/ Assyrian/ Syriac language (modern Aramaic), history and culture."

82 Do children attend Sunday school?

Some are enrolled in weekend education at churches or schools. One purpose of a Catholic education is to prepare students for the sacraments. Latin Rite Catholic children generally make their first communion in the second or third grade. Eastern Rite children are about a year older. Confirmation comes around age 14. However, Chaldean children are confirmed shortly after baptism, so they have no need for sacramental preparation after communion.

83 How do educational levels for Chaldean Americans compare to others?

Because many government jobs were closed to Christians in Iraq, some became lawyers, bankers or engineers there. When they came to the United States, they lacked the certifications and licenses to use their professional skills here. So, they took blue-collar jobs or became entrepreneurs. Chaldeans work to have their children earn college degrees and have careers. According to the 2018 survey commissioned by the Chaldean Community Foundation, 49 percent of heads of households had a bachelor's degree or higher. The 2018 census found 90 percent graduated from high school. This is significantly higher than educational levels for the U.S. population overall.

84 Are education levels rising, then?

Yes. Three surveys for the Chaldean Community Foundation demonstrate this. The 2000 survey reported that 20 percent of heads of households had at least a bachelor's degree. Rates rose to 30 percent in 2008 and 49 percent in 2018. Increasingly, the survey said, Chaldeans are earning professional degrees in medicine, law and engineering.

Chaldean level of education

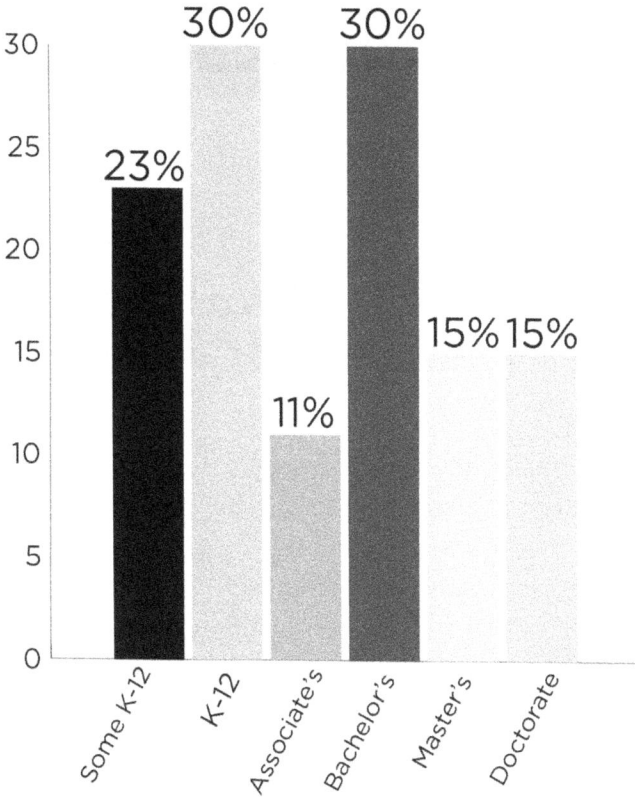

Chart showing Chaldean level of education:
- Some K-12: 23%
- K-12: 30%
- Associate's: 11%
- Bachelor's: 30%
- Master's: 15%
- Doctorate: 15%

Source: Chaldean American Chamber and Chaldean Community Foundation, 2018

Graphic by Alexea Hankin

85 Are some women not allowed to go to college out of state?

This is changing, too. The old ways date to when sons were seen as future breadwinners and daughters were seen as homemakers. Another factor was the desire to keep daughters closer to home. As gender roles have changed for Americans in general and Chaldeans in particular, women's educational options have expanded. ☀

Politics

86 Why did the United States detain several hundred Chaldeans in 2017?

In 2017, President Donald Trump called for a travel ban on seven Muslim countries. One was Iraq. Iraq was exempted from the ban after it agreed to accept 1,400 deportees. The United States then began detaining Iraqis who had committed crimes in the country. Hundreds of Chaldeans were detained. There have been appeals from the Chaldean community and others to free detainees and not deport them to a land that many fled because of hostilities against them.

87 What crimes did detainees commit?

Crimes ranged from shoplifting or staying past an expired visa to felonies, including murder. People had been convicted and either served jail time or were fined. Most crimes were on lesser charges, and many were decades old.

GLOBAL TURMOIL

View video at:
https://www.youtube.com/
watch?v=9P461MxCuNE&

88 How has the community reacted to the detentions?

When Donald Trump ran for office in 2016, he promised to protect Christian minorities. Chaldeans are believed to have given him about 10,000 popular votes in Michigan, which helped him capture the state's Electoral College votes. After he took office and detentions began, some Chaldeans said in news reports that they felt betrayed.

89 What awaits Chaldeans who are deported to Iraq?

Chaldeans said they were worried for their quality of life if they must return to Iraq. Most recent immigrants fled Iraq to escape discrimination and persecution by the government, militias and extremists. Chaldean Americans said deportations would break up families and become "death sentences" for those sent away.

90 How did ISIS treat Chaldeans in Iraq?

ISIS persecuted Chaldeans in Iraq. In Mosul, Chaldeans were told to convert to Islam or be killed. ISIS has changed Iraq's ethnic tapestry forever. It has damaged many religious sites throughout Iraq and Syria and looted or destroyed homes of non-Muslims.

91 How have persecuted or displaced people been affected?

The number of immigrants being accepted into the United States is constantly in flux. Under the Trump Administration, immigration in general has been discouraged. When Iraqi immigration is specifically discouraged, this reduces Chaldean immigration, of course.

92 Have Chaldean Americans held political office?

The first Iraqi-born American to be elected in America was Wadie P. Deddeh, a Chaldean. He served in the California State Assembly from 1967 to 1983. He was a state senator for the next 10 years. Klint Kesto became the first Chaldean elected to the Michigan House of Representatives in 2012. During his second term, Kesto ran unsuccessfully for the Republican nomination for the U.S. Congress. He would have become the first Chaldean American elected to national office.

93 Where are Chaldeans on the U.S. political spectrum?

The Chaldean community leans toward socially conservative ideals and tends to be more pro-business, according to Kesto. Naturally, there are political differences within the community.

94 Are Chaldean Americans active in politics?

Political activity by Chaldean Americans is still developing, according to Kesto and other observers. One reason is that Iraqi immigrants did not experience representative democratic government in Iraq. People who have been discriminated against have trouble trusting government or politics and remain on the sidelines. Chaldeans generally have focused on church, businesses and community rather than politics. ✳

Myths and Stereotypes

95 Do Chaldeans pay taxes?

Yes, they do. The stereotype that they do not has two components. One is the old bias that immigrants come to the United States to collect benefits for which they have not paid any taxes. The fact is, all immigrants pay taxes, but cannot immediately get benefits. Furthermore, most Chaldeans in the United States are citizens. The other part of this stereotype is that, because many Chaldeans own cash businesses, some suppose they dodge taxes. Actually, business owners pay more kinds of taxes than non-business owners and face more regulations.

96 What is the Chaldean mafia?

This term originated among Detroit police in the 1980s and generated some sensationalistic news reports. It referred to a small gang of Chaldean drug dealers. The name implied a level of organization, structure and size that never existed. The gang never had dominance or influence over other gangs, as the Mafia did. The Chaldean gang had no support in the community or homeland. Comprised of some men under the age of 30, it ended with a few killings and some convictions. However, the stereotype made new headlines in 2017 when one of the group's leaders was detained for deportation, 21 years after his murder conviction. The Mafia stereotype, which has been damaging to Italians, falsely suggests an entire ethnic group is involved in crime.

97 Do most Chaldeans own liquor stores or gas stations?

Fifty-eight percent of Chaldeans reported owning one or more businesses in the 2008 community survey, but only 16 percent said it was a convenience store. Just 9 percent reported owning gas stations. While the number of Chaldeans who own such stores is significant, few make their livings this way. According to the survey, "While the stereotype of the Chaldean population by non-Chaldeans is often one of convenience store and gas station owners/ operators, the trend for Generations X and Y is that of high degrees in education and specialization in the law, medicine, finance, accounting and the media."

98 What does "boater" mean?

This derogatory term has been applied to new immigrants from many places. It implies that people arrived on boats, are clinging to the ways of the old country and are not integrating into

American culture. Actually, few immigrants today arrive on boats. The label is more apt to describe ancestors of people whose families have been here for generations. Matthew Stiffler, professor of Arab-American studies at the University of Michigan, told The Arab American News "The term has a negative connotation, even when used in a loving context." People in many cultures have taken over names used against them to counteract the sting. For example, "f.o.b.," meaning "fresh off the boat," became the title of a book in 2015 and then the name of an ABC sitcom. Stiffler advised against using the term boaters at all, even if members of the group say it to each other.

99 Where does the low-education stereotype come from?

This stereotype, like the one about owning convenience stores, is outdated. As research has shown, average education levels are higher for Chaldean adults than they are for the overall population. The education stigma dates to when Chaldeans were new immigrants, learning English and working to survive. The Chaldean community is beyond that stage. There are Chaldean-American student associations on several college campuses, as well as professional associations.

100 Are Chaldeans racially profiled?

In 2017, the ACLU reported on an analysis of 13,000 pages of documents from the Transportation Security Administration. It reported a "disproportionate focus on or an overt bias against Arabs, Muslims, and people of Middle Eastern or South Asian descent." There are no visible distinctions among people of Iraqi descent who are Catholic, Muslim or Christian. In 2017, John Kelly, then secretary of the Department of Homeland Security, said, "I reject anyone that makes that claim" that people are profiled on the basis of religion or color or politics. He was speaking with community activists in Dearborn, Michigan. ☀

Chronology

By Jessica Hanna

940-855 B.C.E. Chaldean tribes migrate to Mesopotamia, the "land between the rivers," meaning the Tigris and Euphrates.

852 B.C.E. Assyrian Empire conquers Chaldeans.

612 B.C.E. Assyrian Empire falls and Chaldean Empire rises with Nabopolassar as king.

605 B.C.E. Nabopolassar dies.

604 B.C.E. Nebuchadnezzar II becomes king and builds the Hanging Gardens of Babylon during his reign.

562 B.C.E. Nebuchadnezzar II dies.

539 B.C.E. Babylon falls to the Persian Empire.

1st Century C.E. Apostles Addai and Mari convert Chaldeans to Christianity.

1553 Pope Julius III recognizes the Chaldean Catholic Church.

1889 Zia Attallah, or Attala, immigrates to Philadelphia and works at a hotel. He later returns to Iraq.

1912-1918 Seeking oil, the British take control of Chaldeans' traditional homeland from the Ottomans and create the State of Iraq.

1917 In Wheeling, West Virginia, Daisy Kory becomes the first Chaldean born in the United States.

1920 Iraqis rebel against the British, who sponsor King Faisal as monarch.

1921 and 1924 The United States passes national origin quotas, limiting immigration.

1923 About 10 Chaldean adults are living in Detroit.

1924-1932 The monarchy leads to Iraqi independence and statehood.

1936-1962 Iraq experiences many revolutions and rebellions.

1938 The first Chaldean grocery store is opened in Detroit.

1940s Chaldeans begin moving to the San Diego area.

1960-1970 The largest wave of Chaldean immigrants comes to America.

1961 The Chaldean American Ladies of Charity is founded in Detroit.

1963-1979 Saddam Hussein and the Baath Party rise to power in Iraq.

1965 U.S. immigration law eliminates national origin, race, and ancestry requirements. Preferences now go to relatives of U.S. citizens, legal permanent residents and highly skilled workers.

1967-1983 Wadie P. Deddeh, the first Iraqi American elected to a statewide office in the United States, serves in the California Assembly and then Senate.

1980-1988 Iran-Iraq war; the United States supports Iraq.

1982 Pope John Paul II chooses Ibrahim N. Ibrahim to be the first Chaldean bishop in the United States and to lead the first diocese in the United States, the

Chaldean Catholic Eparchy of St. Thomas the Apostle. It is headquartered in the Detroit area and covers most of the country.

1990 New U.S. immigration act increases the number of visas for workers and people hoping to become permanent residents.

1990-1991 Iraq invades neighboring Kuwait. The United States defeats Iraq in Operation Desert Storm.

2002 A second Chaldean diocese in the United States is created, the Eparchy of St. Peter the Apostle, with headquarters in San Diego. It covers 19 western states. Sarhad Yawsip Hermiz Jammo, who has worked at the junction of the Chaldean and Assyrian identities, is installed as bishop.

2003-2011 In a new war, the United States invades and occupies Iraq.

2014 Francis Y. Kalabat, who studied in San Diego, is named bishop of the eastern eparchy.

2017 The White House calls for a ban on immigrants from several countries including Iraq, which is taken off the list after a court challenge. Iraq agrees to let the United States send back 1,400 people with criminal convictions. Hundreds of Chaldeans are detained. ☀

Religious Calendar

By Steven Maier

The Chaldean Catholic Church recognizes a solar calendar divided into seasons, each celebrating a different biblical event that established God's relationship with the church.

Subara (4 weeks) – The liturgical narrative begins with a season that many other Christian churches call Advent. It's a time of preparation for the coming Messiah and the birth of Christ.

Denha (7 weeks) – A celebration of God revealed in the flesh as Jesus Christ. It includes the Christmas season.

Soma (7 weeks) – Known as Lent in other Christian traditions, this is a season of fasting and prayer for purification.

Qyamta (7 weeks) – This includes the Easter season. Many Chaldeans stop fasting during this season to celebrate the resurrection of Jesus.

Shleehe (7 weeks) – During this season, Chaldean Catholics celebrate the coming of the Holy Spirit after Pentecost and the empowerment of the apostles who went on to spread Christ's message.

Qayta (7 weeks) – This season points the church toward the purification that Jesus promised and that

Paul preached. It signifies that through trials and condemnation, Christ's followers will be made more holy.

Eliya (7 weeks) – This is the season of Elijah. It is when the church looks back to what the Old Testament prophet said about the end times and the role God's people will play in them.

Qudash idta (4 weeks) – This season draws the liturgical narrative to a close by reminding the church of the kingdom of God in heaven that they will inherit and live in after the end of time.

Like many Christians, Chaldean Catholics recognize Christmas and Easter as the most important holidays in the year. They celebrate the birth of Jesus and his rising from death to life after Roman authorities killed him. On days of celebration, fasting is prohibited.

Other important Chaldean holidays are less familiar to Christians from different denominations. In May, the Feast of Our Lady of the Fields commemorates the end of a famine after farmers asked the Virgin Mary to pray to God to save their crops. Agriculture was a staple of life for Chaldean Catholics in Iraq. This feast venerates Mary under one of her many names. Mary is celebrated extensively throughout the year. May is the month of Mary, and several feasts bear her name or celebrate her rise to heaven. The role of Mary takes on extra meaning for Chaldeans, who revere their mothers as prominent members of their families

The Feast of St. Thomas is celebrated more heavily by Chaldeans than by most American Catholics. It's believed that Thomas, one of the apostles with Jesus at The Last Supper, founded the first churches in India and converted the first Chaldeans to Christianity.

Chaldeans also observe Ba'utha, a three-day fast taking place three weeks before the beginning of Lent. It echoes the people of Nineveh, whom many Chaldeans claim as ancestors. They fasted and mourned for three days to show repentance after the prophet Jonah warned that God would destroy them for their wickedness. Their actions led God to withhold the destruction. The holiday was established more than 1,000 years ago after a five-day fast inspired by the original repentance in Ninevah ended a plague in that area. Approaches to fasting can vary.

Chaldeans also fast on most Fridays and other holidays, including during the Lenten season. Many Chaldeans who observe the Friday fasts simply avoid meat on those days. It's common for Chaldeans to give up something other than food for the seven-week Lenten season. It is more common to fast strictly—with total abstinence from food—at Ba'utha than at other fasting times.

Many Friday fasts recognize saints. Some of the most prominent are the former Chaldean patriarch Mar Shim'un Bar Sabba'e, Mar Hurmiz, Mar Mari and Mar Addai. Mar means "lord" and is a common moniker for saints. Sabba'e was martyred by the ruler of the Iranian empire in 345 in a mass persecution of Christians who refused to convert to Zoroastrianism. The monk Hurmiz founded the Rabban Hurmiz Monastery that was used as the seat of the Chaldean patriarch for some time. Mari and Addai wrote many of the prayers and texts used in the Chaldean Mass.

Chaldeans and other Catholics do not worship saints. Rather, they try to model their lives after them just as the saints modeled their lives after Jesus. Saints are believed to pass prayers on to God and their prayers are likely to secure God's action.

Ba'utha and other somber remembrances are celebrations in a sense, but don't call for greetings like "Happy Easter" or "Merry Christmas." When in doubt, wish Chaldeans a "blessed" Ba'utha or fast day. ☀

Discussion and Reflection

Working on this guide, the authors learned that while each of us has our own beliefs and ideas, we are more alike than we are different. Each of us wants to be free, to be successful, to be accepted and to live our lives authentically. One hundred questions cannot do justice to millennia of history. True understanding does not come with 100 answers, or even 1,000, but each one helps. These questions have been just a start. We hope you use the resources and this discussion guide to keep asking questions as part of a group or in personal reflection.

- The Chaldean identity is woven of several strands. They include religion, language and culture. What are the strands of your identity?
- Iraq, the historic homeland of the Chaldean people, does not welcome them today. How does a disconnect like that affect one's sense of home and national identity?

- Opportunity, flight and family reunification have all driven or drawn Chaldeans to the United States. What were your family's push and pull factors for coming to the United States?
- There can be a struggle between trying to fit into a new home and preserving one's culture. What is gained or lost in this struggle?
- Although Chaldean Americans are a small group nationally, Michigan State decided this guide was needed. Should a group's size determine whether we spend time learning its story?
- Any immigrant family in the United States can have generational differences. What differences have you seen or heard about in your family or others?
- Like other immigrant groups, Chaldeans have been subjected to employment stereotyping. What stereotypes in this guide reminded you of biases about other groups?
- Some Chaldeans work hard to preserve their language. Why is language important?
- Food can be a bridge between cultures or back to one's roots. What did food traditions in this guide remind you about your own family?
- It is natural, when learning about a group of people, to want to have answers that will do for every member of the group. But when people are of different villages or ages, answers diverge. What do differences within groups teach us?
- Take a fresh look at recent news in Iraq but imagine looking at it through the lens of someone who has family there. What further

details would you want in news stories? Where would you find them?

- Some Chaldeans have learned from experience that it is better not to get involved in politics. Can you explain the value of voting in the United States?

Activities

- If you can visit a Chaldean church, attend a service or church event. You will be welcomed.
- Not all Chaldeans live near Chaldean communities. What can you do to show someone isolated from their culture that they are accepted as they are?
- We have seen how food and tea are important parts of Chaldean identity. Break bread with a Chaldean American in their home or yours. If that is not possible, go out to lunch or for tea or coffee. Share some of your food traditions as you learn about theirs.

Remember that when you learn how one person thinks, you know how exactly one person thinks, not the whole group. ✸

Resources

Books

Abraham, Nabeel and Andrew Shryock, eds. Arab Detroit: From Margin to Mainstream. Detroit: Wayne State University Press. 2000.

Asmar, Maria Theresa. Memoirs of a Babylonian Princess (Two volumes and 720 pages). G.B. Zieber & Co. 1844.

Bacall, Jacob. Chaldean Iraqi American Association of Michigan. Mount Pleasant, South Carolina: Arcadia Publishing. 2018.

Bacall, Jacob. Chaldeans in Detroit. Mount Pleasant, South Carolina: Arcadia Publishing. 2014.

Baker, Wayne, Ronald Stockton, Sally Howell, Amaney Jamal, Ann Chic Lin, Andrew Shryock and Mark Tessler. Detroit Arab American Study, 2003. Ann Arbor: Inter-university Consortium for Political and Social Research [distributor], 2006-10-25. http://www.doi.org/10.3886/ICPSR04413.v2

Byle, Joseph James. A Narrative Study of Chaldean Refugees and the Myth of Return: From Chaldean Babylon to the New World, dissertation. Detroit: Wayne State University. 2017. https://digitalcommons.wayne.edu/oa_dissertations/1686. 2017.

Chaldean American Ladies of Charity. Ma Baseema: Middle Eastern Cooking with Chaldean Flair, Ann Arbor: Huron River Press. 2011.

Crichlow, Amanda and Edmund F. McGarrell. Merchants in the Motor City: An Assessment of Arab and Chaldean Business Owners' Perceptions Toward Public Officials and Law Enforcement. Criminology, Criminal Justice Law, & Society, Volume 17, Issue 1, Pages 1-19. 2016.

Hanna-Fatuhi, Amer. The Untold Story of Native Iraqis. Bloomington: Xlibris. 2012.

Hermiz, S.Y., S.Y.H. Jammo, and G.H. Sesi. Chaldeans. The People of Michigan Series. Michigan Ethnic Heritage Studies Center and University of Michigan Ethnic Studies Program. 1983.

Jammo, Sarhad and Andrew Younan. Introductory Chaldean. CreateSpace. 2014.

Namou, Weam. Witnessing a Genocide (Iraqi Americans) (Volume 2) Hermiz Publishing. 2015.

Nasrallah, Nawall. Delights from the Garden of Eden: A Cookbook and a History of the Iraqi Cuisine. Indonesia: Equinox Publishing. 2012.

Perry, Bryon. The Chaldeans: A Contemporary Portrait of One of Civilization's Oldest Cultures. West Bloomfield, Michigan. The Chaldean Cultural Center. 2008.

Sengstock, Mary C. The Chaldean Americans: Changing Conceptions of Ethnic Identity 2nd Edition. Staten Island, New York: Center for Migration Studies, Inc. 1998.

Sengstock, Mary C. Chaldeans in Michigan (Discovering the Peoples of Michigan series) East Lansing: Michigan State University Press. 2005.

Shryock, Andrew, Nabeel Abraham, Sally Howell. Arab Detroit 9/11: Life in the Terror Decade. Detroit: Wayne State University Press. 2011.

Smith, George. The Chaldean Account of Genesis. New York: Scribner, Armstrong & Co., 1876.

Suleiman, Michael. Arabs in America: Building a New Future. Philadelphia: Temple University Press. 1999.

Reports and articles

Chaldean American Ladies of Charity. Chaldean Elders Needs Assessment. Southfield: Area Agency on Aging. 2006. http://www.aaa1b.org/wp-content/uploads/2010/07/Chaldean_report-Final.pdf

Hanoosh, Yasmeen. Minority Identities Before and After Iraq: The Making of the Modern Assyrian and Chaldean Appellations. Arab Studies Journal 24.2 (2016): 8-40. ProQuest.

Hanoosh, Yasmeen. The Politics of Minority Chaldeans Between Iraq and America. ProQuest, 2008. ISBN 0549984755, 9780549984757.

Hanoosh, Yasmeen. Tomorrow They Write their Story: Chaldeans in America and the Transforming Narrative of Identities. Cross / Cultures.115 (2009): 395,421,488. ProQuest.

Levin, Doron P. West Bloomfield Journal: Jews and Ethnic Iraqis: A Neighborhood's Story. The New York Times. December 17, 1990.

Scafe, Marla and Kurt Metzger. The Chaldeans in Metropolitan Detroit. Chaldean American Chamber of Commerce. 2008 Household Survey

Results. http://www.issuu.com/chaldeanchamber/docs/2008chaldeanhouseholdsurvey

Sengstock, Mary C. Chaldean Americans. Countries and their Cultures. World Cultural Encyclopedia. http://www.everyculture.com/multi/Bu-Dr/Chaldean-Americans.html

Chaldean Community Foundation. Chaldeans in Southeast Michigan. 2018. http://www.umdilabs.com/sites/default/files/Chaldean%20Community%20Survey%20Jan%202018.pdf

The Chaldean News regularly publishes about relevant contemporary and historical issues and is available by subscription or at http://www.chaldeannews.com

Denha Garmo, Vanessa. Chaldeans in Michigan: Updated survey shares new data about the community in Metropolitan Detroit. http://www.chaldeannews.com/features-1/2018/2/26/chaldean-in-michigan. 2018.

Denha Garmo, Vanessa. Deadly Detroit: Chaldeans Dying for the American Dream. June 1, 2005.

Denha Garmo, Vanessa. Then and Now: How Chaldean Weddings Have Changed Across Time and Place. http://www.chaldeannews.com/features-1/2018/1/29/then-and-now.

Denha Garmo, Vanessa. Saving the Language of Jesus http://www.chaldeannews.net/saving-the-language-of-jesus. September 26, 2016.

Hanish, Shak. The Chaldean Assyrian Syriac People of Iraq: An Ethnic Identity Problem. Digest of Middle East Studies. 17.1 32-47 (2008): 32-47. http://www.doi.org/10.1111/j.1949-3606.2008.tb00145.x

Harb, Ali. Dearborn. Are Chaldeans Arab? The Arab American News. 2016. http://www.arabamericannews.com/2016/02/19/Are-Chaldeans-Arab/

McWhirter, John. Where Do Languages Go to Die? The tale of Aramaic, a language that once ruled the Middle East and now faces extinction. The Atlantic. September 10, 2015

Rubin, Lori and Navaz Peshotan Bhavnagri. Voices of Recent Chaldean Adolescent Immigrants. Childhood Education. Vol. 77, Issue 5, 2001.

Wegehaupt, Tom: Chaldean community mourns death of patriarch, Melody Farms owner Michael George. The Oakland Press. June 24, 2014. http://www.theoaklandpress.com/obituaries/20140624/chaldean-community-mourns-death-of-patriarch-melody-farms-owner-michael-george

Organizations

Arab American and Chaldean Council, http://www.myacc.org

Catholic Near East Welfare Association (a Vatican agency), http://www.cnewa.org/iraq.html

Chaldean American Association, http://www.chaldeanamerican.org

Chaldean American News, http://www.chaldeannews.com

Chaldean American student associations have been established at Oakland University, Michigan State University, the University of Michigan campuses in Ann Arbor and Dearborn and at Wayne State University.

Chaldean American Association for Health Professionals, http://www.caahp-usa.org

Chaldean American Chamber of Commerce, http://www.chaldeanchamber.com

Chaldean Bar Association, http://www.chaldeanbar.com

Chaldean Catholic Diocese of St. Peter the Apostle, http://www.Kaldu.org and http://www.kaldu.tv/index.html

Chaldean Community Foundation, http://www.chaldeanfoundation.org

Chaldean Cultural Center, http://www.chaldeanculturalcenter.org

Chaldean Educational Center of America, http://www.chaldean4u.org

Chaldean Heritage Foundation, http://www.chaldeanheritage.org

Chaldean Iraqi American Association of Michigan

The Chaldean News http://www.chaldeannews.com

Chaldean Voice Radio, http://www.chaldeanvoice.com

Chaldean Youth Camp, http://www.chaldeanyouthcamp.org

Keys Grace Academy, http://www.keysacademies.com

Mother of God Chaldean Catholic Church, http://www.ourladyofchaldeans.com

St. Thomas the Apostle Chaldean Catholic Eparchy of the U.S.A. http://www.chaldeanchurch.com

United Community Family Services (Chaldean American Ladies of Charity), http://www.calconline.org ☀

Our Story

The 100 Questions and Answers series springs from the idea that good journalism should increase cross-cultural competence and understanding. Most of our guides are created by Michigan State University journalism students.

We use journalistic interviews to surface the simple, everyday questions that people have about each other but might be afraid to ask. We use research and reporting to get the answers and then put them where people can find them, read them and learn about each other.

These cultural competence guides are meant to be conversation starters. We want people to use these guides to get some baseline understanding and to feel comfortable asking more questions. We put a resources section in every guide we make and we arrange community conversations. While the guides can answer questions in private, they are meant to spark discussions.

Making these has taught us that people are not that different from each other. People share more similarities than differences. We all want the same things for ourselves and for our families. We want to be accepted, respected and understood.

Please email your thoughts and suggestions to Series Editor Joe Grimm at joe.grimm@gmail.com, at the Michigan State University School of Journalism.

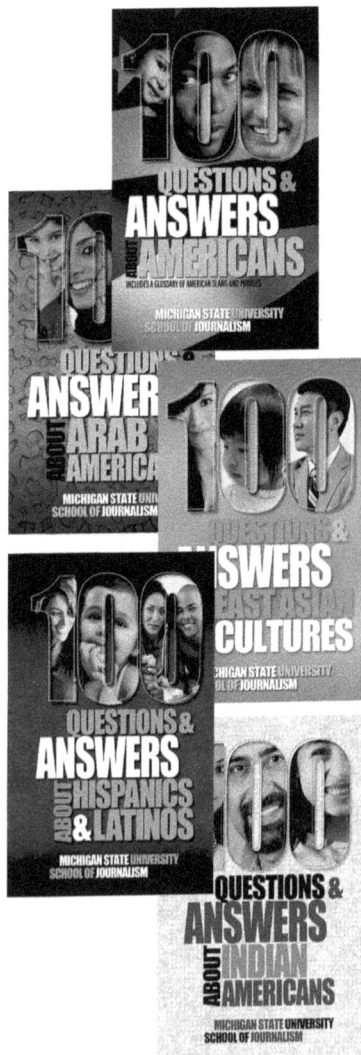

http://news.jrn.msu.edu/culturalcompetence

Related Books

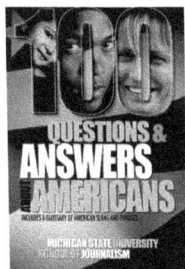

100 Questions and Answers About Americans
Michigan State University School of Journalism, 2013
This guide answers some of the first questions asked by newcomers to the United States. Questions represent dozens of nationalities coming from Africa, Asia, Australia, Europe and North and South America. Good for international students, guests and new immigrants.
http://news.jrn.msu.edu/culturalcompetence/

ISBN: 978-1-939880-20-8

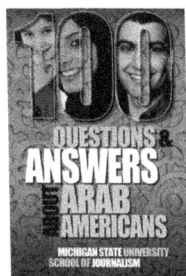

100 Questions and Answers About Arab Americans
Michigan State University School of Journalism, 2014
The terror attacks of Sept. 11, 2001, propelled these Americans into a difficult position where they are victimized twice. The guide addresses stereotypes, bias and misinformation. Key subjects are origins, religion, language and customs. A map shows places of national origin.
http://news.jrn.msu.edu/culturalcompetence/

ISBN: 978-1-939880-56-7

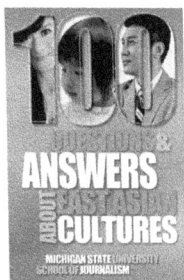

100 Questions and Answers About East Asian Cultures
Michigan State University School of Journalism, 2014
Large university enrollments from Asia prompted this guide as an aid for understanding cultural differences. The focus is on people from China, Japan, Korea and Taiwan and includes Mongolia, Hong Kong and Macau. The guide includes history, language, values, religion, foods and more.
http://news.jrn.msu.edu/culturalcompetence/

ISBN: 978-939880-50-5

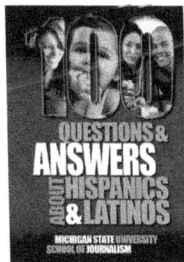

100 Questions and Answers About Hispanics & Latinos
Michigan State University School of Journalism, 2014
This group became the largest ethnic minority in the United States in 2014 and this guide answers many of the basic questions about it. Questions were suggested by Hispanics and Latinos. Includes maps and charts on origin and size of various Hispanic populations.
http://news.jrn.msu.edu/culturalcompetence/

ISBN: 978-1-939880 44-4

Print and ebooks available on Amazon.com and other retailers.

Related Books

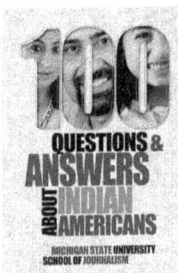

100 Questions and Answers About Indian Americans
Michigan State University School of Journalism, 2013
In answering questions about Indian Americans, this guide also addresses Pakistanis, Bangladeshis and others from South Asia. The guide covers religion, issues of history, colonization and national partitioning, offshoring and immigration, income, education, language and family.
http://news.jrn.msu.edu/culturalcompetence/

ISBN: 978-1-939880-00-0 m

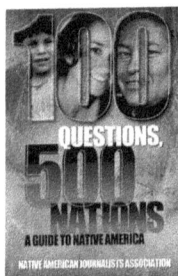

100 Questions, 500 Nations: A Guide to Native America
Michigan State University School of Journalism, 2014
This guide was created in partnership with the Native American Journalists Association. The guide covers tribal sovereignty, treaties and gaming, in addition to answers about population, religion, U.S. policies and politics. The guide includes the list of federally recognized tribes.
http://news.jrn.msu.edu/culturalcompetence/

ISBN: 978-1-939880-38-3

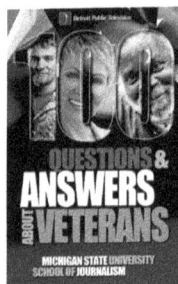

100 Questions and Answers About Veterans
Michigan State University School of Journalism, 2015
This guide treats the more than 20 million U.S. military veterans as a cultural group with distinctive training, experiences and jargon. Graphics depict attitudes, adjustment challenges, rank, income and demographics. Includes six video interviews by Detroit Public Television.
http://news.jrn.msu.edu/culturalcompetence/

ISBN: 978-1-942011-00-2

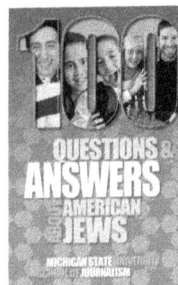

100 Questions and Answers About American Jews
Michigan State University School of Journalism 2016
We begin by asking and answering what it means to be Jewish in America. The answers to these wide-ranging, base-level questions will ground most people and set them up for meaningful conversations with Jewish acquaintances.
http://news.jrn.msu.edu/culturalcompetence/

ISBN: 978-1-942011-22-4

Print and ebooks available on Amazon.com and other retailers.

Related Books

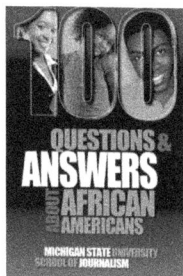

100 Questions and Answers About African Americans
Michigan State University School of Journalism, 2016
Learn about the racial issues that W.E.B. DuBois said in 1900 would be the big challenge for the 20th century. This guide explores Black and African American identity, history, language, contributions and more. Learn more about current issues in American cities and campuses.
http://news.jrn.msu.edu/culturalcompetence/

ISBN: 978-1-942011-19-4

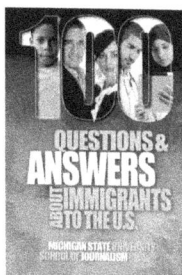

100 Questions and Answers About Immigrants to the U.S.
Michigan State University School of Journalism 2016
This simple, introductory guide answers 100 of the basic questions people ask about U.S. immigrants and immigration in everyday conversation. It has answers about identity, language, religion, culture, customs, social norms, economics, politics, education, work, families and food.

ISBN: 978-1-934879-63-4

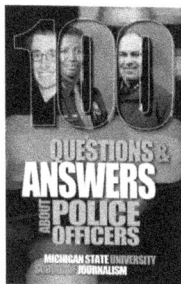

100 Questions and Answers about Police Officers
Michigan State University School of Journalism 2018
This simple, introductory guide answers 100 of the basic questions people ask about police officers, sheriff's deputies, public safety officers and tribal police. It focuses on policing at the local level, where procedures vary from coast to coast. The guide includes a resource about traffic stops.

ISBN: 978-1-64180-013-6

Print and ebooks available on Amazon.com and other retailers.

* 9 7 8 1 6 4 1 8 0 0 4 1 9 *